To:

From:

outcomes. Paul has a gift for boiling any skill down to the five to seven key ideas that are critical to keep in one's awareness. He communicates these ideas in a clear, concise fashion, which makes them easy to put to use. I have been waiting impatiently for this book so that all of Paul's ideas about conducting more effective meetings would be in one place. I am eager to share this valuable resource with my clients.

—Lynda Rands, executive coach, WorkLife Resources

Paul came into our leadership team and taught us how to make a significant return on our business by creating a productive and rewarding environment for our division of 160 employees. Paul's teaching was, by far, the best educational experience I have had. (And I achieved my undergraduate in engineering at Carnegie Mellon University and my masters in management at MIT.)

—Charles Hura, business consultant

Meetings can be a mind-numbing squandering of time, money, patience, and other finite resources. But they needn't and shouldn't be. In *Meetings Matter*, Paul Axtell shows how thoughtful, respectful, and focused conversation is the key to effective meetings. What's more, he provides lots of specific strategies and tactics. Adopt the practices suggested here and the meetings you attend will never be fruitless again. The bonus? You and your colleagues will be more engaged than ever in producing great results.

—Rodger Dean Duncan, author of
Change-Friendly Leadership

I have been following Paul's teaching in organizations for more than a decade now. The essence is: When people matter, things get done, and they get done in amazing ways!

—Audie Penn, master black belt,
Caterpillar Global Deployment

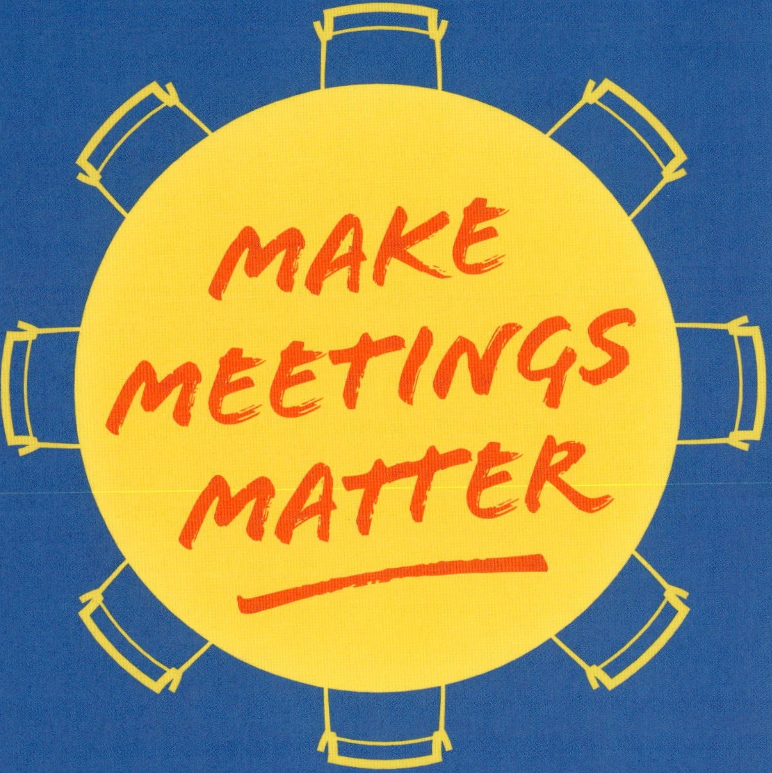

MAKE MEETINGS MATTER

How to Turn Meetings from Status Updates to Remarkable Conversations

PAUL AXTELL

Photo Credits
Internal images © pages viii, 3, 18, 52, 73, 74, 95, Westend61/Getty Images; page 10,
TARIK KIZILKAYA/Getty Images; page 27, Maskot/Getty Images; page 28, visualspace/
Getty Images; page 34, Prathan Chorruangsak/EyeEm/Getty Images; page 40, kzenon/
Getty Images; page 47, moodboard/Getty Images; page 60, Wathna Racha/EyeEm/
Getty Images; pages 86, 124, piranka/Getty Images; page 96, Hero Images/Getty
Images; page 112, Willie B. Thomas/Getty Images
Internal images on pages xv, xvi, 9, 39, 68, 102, and 127 have been provided by
Unsplash; these images are licensed under CC0 Creative Commons and have been
released by the author for public use.

Published by Simple Truths, an imprint of Sourcebooks
P.O. Box 4410, Naperville, Illinois 60567-4410
(630) 961-3900
sourcebooks.com

This edition is based on *Meetings Matter*, originally published in
2015 in the United States of America by Jackson Creek Press.

Printed and bound in China.
OGP 10 9 8 7 6 5 4 3 2 1

For Amy, Jesse, and Cindy.

I wrote this book for everyone who wants to be really good, for everyone who wants their organization to be successful, and especially for those who have endured countless meetings wishing they would be better and not quite sure what to do about them.

You and your meetings can be beyond good.

Contents

Preface

This book is about getting twenty people in a meeting to feel like five friends having a conversation over coffee. Not easy, but doable.

As a manager, would it make a difference if employees looked forward to your meetings? As an individual, would it help if you knew that every meeting on your schedule this week would add momentum to your priorities and projects?

Meetings are a competitive edge for every organization that gets them right. And for individuals, the ability to lead and participate effectively in meetings is at the heart of having influence in an organization.

Like anything worthy of mastery, it takes patience, persistence, and practice to take your meetings from ordinary to extraordinary. But it will not take years. Choosing a single thing to focus on in your next five to ten meetings will produce immediate change. This book sets you on the right trajectory. In three months, your meetings can be dramatically different.

Introduction

The ability to set up a conversation, manage the conversation, and wrap it up effectively is the missing piece in meetings everywhere. While most people think passion, knowledge, and drive are all they need to succeed, through my long career in organizational management, I am here to tell you: **it is your meeting skills that will set you apart**. Collectively, any organization that establishes a deep capacity for excellent meetings will have an edge in execution, accomplishment, and engagement.

Despite solutions being quite simple at their core, meetings continue to be a source of irritation and frustration—especially when people end up taking work home to make up for time lost in unproductive meetings. These are the six most common complaints:

1. My boss is terrible at leading meetings.

2. A few people dominate the conversations.

3. The group is too large to get anything done.

4. We just pass along information. We don't talk about real issues.

5. Too many people are distracted by devices.

6. We don't make progress between meetings.

The online meeting scheduling firm Doodle found these to be the most prevalent irritants:

Biggest irritations in meetings:

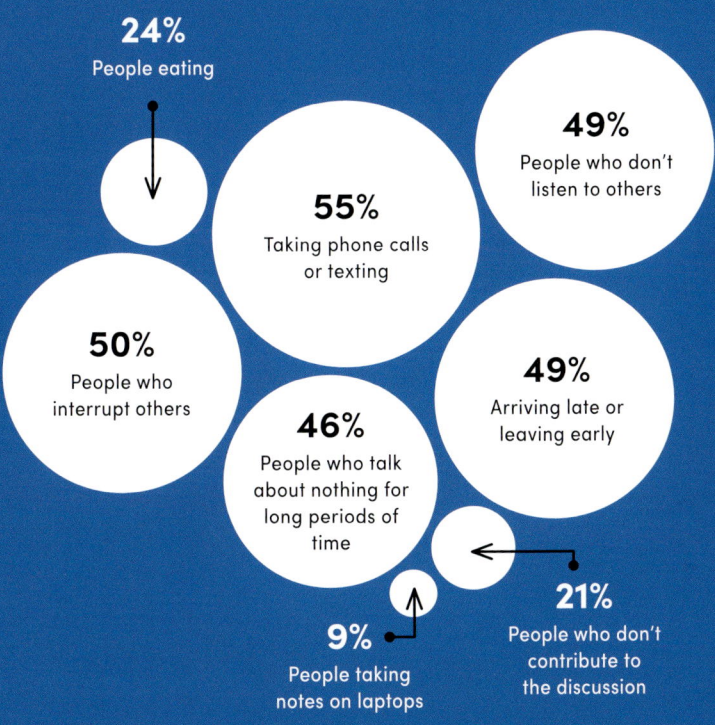

24%
People eating

55%
Taking phone calls
or texting

49%
People who don't
listen to others

50%
People who
interrupt others

46%
People who talk
about nothing for
long periods of
time

49%
Arriving late or
leaving early

9%
People taking
notes on laptops

21%
People who don't
contribute to
the discussion

The Doodle State of Meetings Report 2019, from research with 6,528
professionals in the UK, Germany, and the USA

Given this broad list of complaints, it's no wonder most people have given up hope that things could be different. Good people are no longer preparing for meetings or participating in ways that add value. They have moved to the sidelines.

This book will provide you the tools to solve each of these complaints. **It's time to move meetings from frustrating to effective to remarkable.** The ideas in this book work, and their impact will reach far beyond your meetings. The foundational ideas on perspective, conversation, and relationship will change your interactions with your family and colleagues and impact almost everything you do.

If we can make each of our conversations richer in terms of engagement, attention, candor, and respect, our meetings will improve.

1

Choose the Perspective: This Matters

When you change the way you look at things, the things you look at change.

—DR. WAYNE DYER

The first step on the journey toward effective meetings begins with choosing empowering new perspectives. Much of this book focuses on the techniques and practices required to make your meetings better. Unfortunately, even the best tactics cannot overcome a *dis*empowering perspective.

We all operate with certain perspectives in place—values we learned from our parents, from our coaches, from friends, or from lines in movies or books that resonated with our thoughts about ourselves or about life. Such phrases remind us of who we want to be or how we want to respond to life. Here are two that have stuck with me:

▶ From Adam Wainwright, St. Louis Cardinals pitcher: "You fall into the trap of being mediocre. If you're OK with being mediocre, then you're going to be mediocre."

▶ From Sir Edmund Hillary, New Zealand mountaineer: "People do not decide to become extraordinary. They decide to accomplish extraordinary things."

These two broad perspectives point us forward. Simply noticing where we have settled for mediocre meetings and choosing to get on the path of being extraordinary will bring immediate change. In addition, throughout the book are perspectives that, if chosen and embraced, will impact your group's conversations. For example, as the person calling the meeting, **you are responsible for the time and talent in the room; do not disrespect it**. Or, as a participant, **your participation could make all the difference in the outcomes and experience of this meeting**.

Perspectives shape our experience—of life and meetings

A perspective for everyday life: Treat each person, each conversation, and each moment as though they matter

This is perhaps the most powerful perspective for shaping a positive experience in many aspects of life and work. You may be familiar with Tolstoy's story "The Three Questions" from *What Men Live By*:

1 Where is the most important place?

2 When is the most important time?

3 Who is the most important person?

The answers are, of course:

1 Right here.

2 Right now.

3 The person you're with.

The point is to treat everything as though it matters and give your full attention to whatever you are doing and to whomever you are with right now. It's easy to slip into dealing with certain tasks or situations mindlessly; we all do it. If you have been going through life this way, there is a tremendous upside to beginning to treat what you do as if it matters. If you are attentive and engaged in the moment, those around you will notice. In a world of devices and multitasking, attention is often fleeting. The key is to be present, attentive, and engaged.

This is not a new idea. The adage "if it's worth doing, it's worth doing right" has been with us for a long time.

Adopting a new perspective changes behavior

A research laboratory asked me to conduct interpersonal skills training for their security guards because of visitor complaints about how they'd been treated. Before I designed the training, I sat down with the guards and asked what they thought they needed. Their reactions were enlightening: "No one told us about the complaints!" and "What do they want us to be, receptionists or security guards?"

Then one guard said, "We can welcome people. We don't need any training. *Someone just needed to tell us that our job has two parts: provide security for the facility and make people feel like guests.* We can do this." Everyone agreed, and the complaints went to zero.

Find a new mindset for meetings

Some of the most troubling perspectives for meetings are ones we have drifted into over time without thinking about it. If you pay attention, you'll hear people expressing, almost without realizing it, a series of comments about meetings that are not positive.

This becomes a self-fulfilling prophecy, and meetings are almost doomed from the start. Here are two perspectives that provide a refreshing starting point for meetings. First, **meetings matter**—they are high-leverage events at the heart of effective organizations. Second, **choose ownership for each meeting you attend**.

On a recent visit to a corporate office building, I saw a series of images of employees with the phrase, "I own the moment." This single phrase captures two powerful ideas: being present and being responsible. Each will have an impact if you apply them to meetings. For example, if everyone treated each meeting as if it were their own and walked in looking for what they might do to make it successful, your meetings would improve.

A final perspective: This shall be

One of the fundamental variables in whether your meetings improve is how determined you are that they change. I love the term *intention* when it means "this shall be." Intention is different from a New Year's resolution, which tends to be treated as a wish—hoped for but quickly forgotten in the demands of daily life.

Knowing you want something is not the same as being intentional about making it happen. This book shows you how to design, lead, and participate in meetings to make a difference. The question is, will you make it happen? It's not that difficult. Just take it one idea at a time, one meeting at a time.

TRY THIS

→ *Slow down, do one thing at a time, and treat this person, this conversation, this activity as if it matters.*

→ *Find a phrase that captures the new mindset you want for meetings.*

→ *Collect seven phrases that help you to be at your best.*

If you don't like something, change it. If you can't change it, change your attitude.

—MAYA ANGELOU, AMERICAN POET

2

Master Effective Conversation

Conversation is at the heart of being effective

It's so easy to take something for granted until you don't have it—like breathing, until you suddenly can't catch your breath. Conversation is like that. Conversations are the threads that weave the fabric of our lives, yet we don't pay attention until they're unraveling.

We work on specialized conversations—presentation skills, negotiating skills, sales approaches, conflict

Each conversation we have with our coworkers, customers, significant others, and children either enhances those relationships, flatlines them, or takes them down. Given this, what words or level of attention do you wish to bring to your conversations with the people who are most important to you?

—SUSAN SCOTT, *FIERCE CONVERSATIONS*

resolution. We have not been students of how to be great with people by paying attention to how we converse with each other. We tend to take conversation for granted.

Yet we raise kids with conversations. Relationships are created and shaped by conversations. Having influence in an organization depends on social skills and meeting skills. And we also know the impact of gossip and other disempowering conversations that are not worth having. The quality of our conversations matters.

Making conversations work

If you embrace the importance of conversation, then you can focus on noticing what it takes to make every conversation work out as intended. These are the fundamental practices for effective conversation:

▶ Put the rest of the world on hold and devote yourself to the person you are with.

▶ Listen in a way that encourages others to keep speaking.

▶ Be aware of what you say and how you say it.

Listening is a fine art... and often missing

One of the most influential articles I've read was about listening. From American journalist Brenda Ueland's book *Strength to Your Sword Arm*, the article described what magical things happen when someone is speaking in the presence of a person who knows how to listen without interruption or without changing the conversation—someone who can listen whole-heartedly and then, when needed, add the supportive request, "**Tell me more**."

Of course, there are times when good conversation is a back-and-forth affair, even a bit chaotic. However, underlying those conversations is the notion of being *able* to slow down and just listen. Often that's all people need—to be heard, to *feel* heard. People are willing to be expressive and vulnerable if they sense that we are listening in an attentive way.

Years ago, I taught a program called "A Special Evening on Listening" for some of my corporate clients and their families. During the session, we did an exercise in which the person listening could not say anything at all. It's an exercise in devoting your complete attention to the person who is speaking so he or she truly feels heard. A couple of weeks later, I received an email from Andrea, one of the participants:

Last night, my fourteen-year-old daughter, Chelsea, came home and said, "Mom, I need to talk. If you can listen to me the way we learned the other evening, you can save me a three-mile bicycle ride to my friend's house." Thank you!

Michael P. Nichols, author of *The Lost Art of Listening*, makes the point that just listening without adding to or changing the conversation is what is important. **Reassuring someone isn't listening. Trying to solve the problem isn't listening. Just listening is listening.**

Yet we don't listen very often, at least not in a way that is meaningful. We interrupt. We finish other people's sentences. We pretend to listen. And certainly, we are not thinking about the impact of our listening on the conversation or the other person.

Attention and caring are tightly connected. If you pay attention to someone who is speaking in a meeting, they will interpret this to mean that you care. If the top person constantly checks a device or engages in side conversations, people get the impression that their speaking or the topic being discussed is not important.

> ## The meaning of your communication is the response you get.
>
> **—RICHARD BANDLER AND JOHN GRINDER, AMERICAN AUTHORS**

Be responsible for how you speak

Consider this point of view: you are responsible not only for what you say but for how it is received. No one expects this of you, but it is a high standard you can set for yourself.

Being easy to work with is part of building trust. Reflecting on these questions will help you identify where you might improve:

▶ What conversations do people associate with you?

▶ Do you lean toward speaking first or listening?

▶ Do people feel that you are truly interested in them?

Think about mistakes you might be making that can detract from someone's experience of being with you, such as:

▶ Hijacking every conversation, having it be about you

▶ Speaking more often or longer than people can tolerate

▶ Introducing negative conversations into the organization

▶ Making negative comments about someone who is not present

The goal is to speak and listen in a way that has people looking forward to spending time with you, in a way that leads to trust and respect.

Four Cs to look for

Effective conversation has four elements: **clarity, candor, commitment, and completion**. A conversation may seem fine, but then you later discover the intended actions or the expected alignment did not occur. When a conversation does not have the desired result, one of these pieces is likely missing.

I love this simple and elegant model because it gives you four things to pay attention to in all conversations.

Check for clarity

It might not be obvious when clarity is missing in a conversation, but lack of clarity is responsible for many misunderstandings and mistakes.

Clarity requires back-and-forth conversation, so establishing safety and encouraging people to ask questions is important. So is scheduling enough time for each topic so that people will ask their questions. Also, be careful about using PowerPoint, because this tends to create a passive audience and stifle questions.

Clarity provides the basis for understanding, alignment, and engagement. Don't assume that you have it. Check often by asking, "Is everyone clear? Anyone need more explanation?"

> **I've found that if I say what I'm really thinking and feeling, people are more likely to say what they really think and feel. The conversation becomes a real conversation.**
>
> —CAROL GILLIGAN, AMERICAN PSYCHOLOGIST

Speak with candor

Candor means being authentic—saying what you mean and meaning what you say. Candor is a key element of groups that work well together. It's part of relationships that are special. Life is difficult enough without wondering about what your colleagues or friends really think.

A colleague shared a story of a senior manager who always brings his people together for a "no secrets" meeting when he conducts facility visits. He wants to know how people are doing, how projects are progressing, and what people need in terms of support and resources. Each of these questions are put into play:

▶ What would you like to ask me?

▶ What do you think I need to know?

▶ Where are you struggling?

▶ What are you proud of?

Great questions, but even greater because this manager's invitation to a "no secrets" conversation signals that his people have permission to ask and share anything they want. Of course, it helps that this manager is sincere, authentic, and caring, which creates the trust and safety this kind of conversation requires.

Ask for specific commitments

If you commit to taking action by a specific date, it is much more likely to happen than if the action is simply added to your list of things to do.

People are more productive when facing deadlines. Still, leaders don't ask for this kind of specific commitment because they think it might be interpreted as micromanaging or a lack of trust.

One of the keys to project management is being specific about what will be done, when it will be done, and who will do it. I use the expression *X by Y or call*. You're asking someone to do task X by date Y and, if something gets in the way of fulfilling that commitment, to agree in advance to pick up the phone and call you.

Check for completion

This means not changing topics until all parties are ready to end the discussion. This also ensures that no critical point or question is left unexpressed. "Does anyone have anything else to say or ask?" "I'm ready to change topics; is everyone okay with that?" Checking to see if everyone is ready to leave a topic will reveal issues that might interfere with clarity and alignment.

Conversation shapes our world

Conversations shape who we are. Most people can identify decisions they made about themselves early in life based on what they were told or what was said in their presence. You can most likely recall a time when someone—a boss, a parent, a friend—had a conversation with you that you still remember, one that helped determine who you are today.

Conversations also shape our families and the cultures within which we work. What conversations take place around you? How do these conversations define the organization? Are they moving the organization forward or getting in the way?

Day in and day out, most people simply don't think about their conversations. Consider that every conversation can be enhanced—sometimes with more careful listening, sometimes by removing distractions, sometimes by inviting new voices into the conversation. You have something to say about each conversation in which you participate and therefore with every person you touch each day.

Conversation matters.

TRY THIS

→ *Listen longer. Speak in a way that is clear and concise.*

→ *Notice when commitments are made without dates. Add dates.*

→ *After speaking in a meeting, reflect on what you said and how you said it.*

Each person's life is lived as a series of conversations.

—DEBORAH TANNEN, AMERICAN LINGUISTICS PROFESSOR

3

Create Supportive Relationships

I want it to matter that we met.

—MINDY HALL, AMERICAN AUTHOR

I love this quote. When I remember it, I'm more interested and attentive when I sit down next to you in a meeting or in the stands at a sporting event. With respect to creating and enhancing relationships, it's a game changer. If you adopt this perspective, you will end up knowing more people in a more profound way.

The effectiveness of any meeting is determined by the quality of the relationships among the people who walk into the room. Meetings with four or five colleagues who trust and respect each other are easy. To get the same level of conversation with larger groups, it's imperative to get to know each other in a way that gives you permission to say or ask anything, in a way that makes challenging, back-and-forth conversation safe.

Building relationships is part of the job

Your ability to work on cross-functional teams, in matrix organizations, or across organizational boundaries is enhanced by knowing lots of people. Part of working in an organization demands that you find time to create and maintain the relationships you need to be successful.

With today's hurry-up pace, we've lost the notion of making time for other people. Events designed to get employees together after work no longer hold the same interest. We eat at our desks, decline invitations for coffee, and rush to get home.

There is something about an invitation to have coffee that signals a genuine interest in connecting with the other person. And those connections forged over coffee, tea, or lunch impact your ability to get things done in the organization.

I'm not talking about a huge time investment here. Thirty minutes, once a week, and you could make new connections or deepen your relationship with fifty colleagues in a year's time.

Create trusting relationships

A client once asked if I could help his management team and the union reps figure out how to work toward resolving issues. Both sides thought the problem was a lack of trust. I provided an exercise to begin each weekly meeting with three rounds of one-on-one listening. One person spoke to a question for three minutes while the other person just listened—no questions or comments. Then they exchanged roles for another three minutes. We used questions like these:

▶ Tell me about the neighborhood in which you grew up.

▶ What are you working on or learning that has you excited?

▶ What can you tell me about yourself that might make it easier to understand you and work with you?

The exercise is designed around two fundamental ideas: attentive listening allows people to be more expressive and authentic, and if people talk about things that matter to them, the chances of creating connection increase dramatically.

This time spent getting to know one another was enough to create a level of trust that changed how they spoke and listened to each other in their negotiations. **No special team-building events required.**

Use meetings to build your network

Your meetings can be a primary place to build and enhance your network of relationships—the relationships that will allow you to be successful not only in meetings but with every aspect of your work in the organization.

Traditionally, we think of working the room as the act of circulating among people at a large gathering. Here are seven ways to work the room in meetings:

1. **Take the initiative.** Make connecting with people your focus as you walk in. Listen throughout the meeting for what you can learn about people.

2 **Arrive early and stay late.** Introduce yourself to anyone you don't already know. Catch up with people you haven't seen for a while. Ask about their projects, their trips, interests, and their families.

3 **Greet people as they arrive.** Don't worry about having a conversation with everyone, but do quickly connect, even if it is just saying their names and nodding at them across the table. Look for new people and welcome them.

4 **Ask people to share about things that matter to them.** You can show interest in a person without crossing personal boundaries. Be curious and sincere, and it will work out.

5 **Be interested.** Keep your focus on the other person's conversation. Resist the temptation to turn the conversation to yourself. You must share occasionally to make this a partnership, but err on the side of listening rather than speaking.

6 **Use people's names.** Ask if you don't remember. Confident people acknowledge when they've forgotten. Plus, if you don't remember, it is likely they don't either!

7 **Afterward, make notes on people you meet and what you discuss.** This serves you in two ways: you will remember more, and the notes can serve to refresh your memory before future meetings.

Overcome common connection hurdles

Here is a set of some standard problems in creating connections, along with solutions you can enact at any time:

▶ **When do I find the time?** Luckily, the gift you offer when you ask people how their kids did in the weekend soccer games takes only a few minutes. If you listen flat out for three or four minutes, the conversation will have greater impact than this small investment of time suggests. People can say a lot in a few minutes if you just listen.

▶ **How do I get comfortable meeting people?** If you're not already comfortable meeting people and engaging in conversation, you're not alone. But comfort is not a prerequisite. You can master working the room, and if you work in a large organization and want to be a solid contributor, it's required! With practice, your confidence will increase, and so will your comfort level.

▶ **How do I start a conversation with someone I don't know?** Start by simply being curious about people. Give yourself permission to ask questions. Think beyond typical questions such as *How are you doing?* or *What's your job?* Instead, a request like *Tell me about the projects you are working on that you are excited about* will elicit a conversation that is richer, more specific, and easier for them to talk about. *What is your story?* is one of my favorite starters. The point is to transcend the superficial.

▶ **How can I do this authentically?** At first, anything you try to change feels awkward. If your intention is to find a way to get into an interesting conversation with people, then it is authentic.

▶ **What do I say when people ask me questions?**
Being able to talk on demand is a critical skill. When
you are invited into a conversation, learn to respond
in a meaningful way. When someone asks *How was
your weekend?* share how it was or what you did.
Don't take twenty minutes, but do share what you
most enjoyed. Then reciprocate: "Thanks for asking.
I'd like to hear about your weekend." The idea is to
be genuine and friendly, not brilliant and captivating.

▶ **Do I have to be friends with everyone?** We all
have different definitions of what it means to be
friends, but if you are going to work together, why
not interact in a way that builds connection?

TRY THIS

→ *Listen for what you can learn about people in each meeting.*

→ *Leave each meeting with the name of someone with whom to
follow up.*

→ *Create a goal of connecting with four new people each month.*

The conversation is the relationship.

—DAVID WHYTE, ENGLISH POET

4

Decide What Matters and Who Cares

Never underestimate what might happen if people who care talk about things that matter.

—LARRY ROPER, AMERICAN ACADEMIC

Well-run meetings allow you and your team to clarify issues, set direction, and make progress. Meetings are essential to your team's success. And yet there never seems to be a wealth of effective meetings in any organization. When you are thoughtful about choosing what makes it onto the agenda and whom to invite, people will look forward to attending. Here's why:

▶ If you limit your meetings to discussions about important issues, your meetings will have more impact.

▶ If you invite only those required, the conversations will be focused and productive.

▶ You will protect people's time, making sure the investment value is high for those attending and giving those not attending more time for individual work.

Be vigilant about what gets on the agenda

I remember asking the CEO of a Fortune 100 company to speak at a leadership seminar. He pulled open his desk drawer and took out a list. "I appreciate the invitation. I'm sure the seminar is worthwhile. But this is how I decide where I am going to put my time and energy. This is my list of imperatives for the year. If you can show me how speaking at your event will forward one or more of these imperatives, I'll do it. If you can't, I won't."

Most managers and leadership teams could benefit from this kind of rigor in deciding what gets their time and attention in meetings. Otherwise, why meet?

Are you honoring the time of group members by discussing issues that require their thinking, alignment, and action? It's an important question, and in my experience, few groups could answer in the affirmative. If you want to meet on a regular basis, fine. Just make sure you are thoughtful about the agenda for each meeting and cancel if it doesn't respect the time and talent in the room.

Schedule fewer topics and more time for each topic

A good guideline is two topics per hour. Schedule enough time to discuss the topic, reach alignment, and agree on next steps. The criteria remain the same regardless of the meeting topic: Are you doing complete work on each topic? Does each conversation lead to clarity and alignment about what happens next?

Invite only the people who must be there

This is the "who cares" part of the question: Whose presence is necessary for the topics to be fully addressed? Who, if they can't attend, means you might as well reschedule?

Once you have the core group committed to

attending, you can ask if there is anyone else with an interest or potential contribution who merits an invitation. Invite people:

▶ With organizational knowledge who can point out flaws in your approach

▶ Whose support will be vital during execution

▶ Who have a perspective that no one else in the room can represent

▶ Who are new to the organization and would benefit by being included

▶ Who have concerns about the project and being part of the conversation would be the most effective way to alleviate those concerns

Inclusion is important, but so is remembering that

one of the common complaints about meetings is that there are people attending who are not relevant to the topic.

Eight is the target number

A Fortune 500 CEO made a powerful statement that makes sense to most of us: "I find it easier to be myself in small groups."

Stanford management science and organizational behavior professor Robert Sutton wrote a blog post, titled "Why Big Teams Suck," about the troubles that arise when groups get too large: "It is difficult, perhaps downright impossible, to have a coherent and emotionally satisfying conversation that engages each member of the party all at once. Typically, the group breaks into a series of smaller conversations or a few people do all the talking and the others say little or nothing."

Five to eight is best for most working groups— small enough to sit in physical proximity, get everyone's views considered, and assure a candid and authentic

conversation. Plus, being thoughtful about who should attend each meeting will mean fewer meetings for many people!

Question the necessity to attend

Look at the meetings you have scheduled for this week. Does every meeting honor you and your priorities? If not, find a way to decline while still supporting the person who called the meeting.

Keith is a senior executive who asked for help in making time for four new goals. I told him to carve eight hours out of his current weekly schedule to devote substantial time to these projects. He thought it was impossible until his assistant said, "I can do that for you. You are in fifteen hour-long meetings every week. Let me tell them they get you for thirty minutes, and they decide what part of the meeting they want you for or whether you need to attend at all."

It never occurred to this senior manager to question his time in meetings. He also sent a communication to his organization letting them know they had permission to do the same.

Part of being an effective meeting participant is realizing that you have the right to ask for what you need, and that includes questioning whether you must attend. Sure, there are some meetings you won't be able to decline. But most managers will be supportive if you choose to protect your time without diminishing your value to any group to which you belong.

If you choose not to attend, you have certain responsibilities to the group and to the person leading the meeting. These include:

▶ Giving your input to someone who will be attending

▶ Asking someone to take notes and let you know what happened

▶ Giving the leader permission to assign you work

▶ Agreeing to align with any decisions that are made

You get the idea: if you don't attend, you are still responsible for making the meeting successful. In the same way, give your people permission to question whether their attendance is necessary or to protect their time. You might also think about when you schedule meetings and avoid disrupting people during their most productive or creative times of day.

Ensure that people not attending stay informed

If you are more thoughtful about whom you invite—erring on the side of fewer people—you want to think about those who are not invited. Beforehand, tell those not invited about the meeting so they can provide input or make a case for attending. During the meeting, keep their interests in mind. Afterward, consider who would like to know about what was discussed and decided. Lastly, prepare a summary of the meeting that takes care of the needs of people who do not attend.

TRY THIS

→ *Review your agenda topics for the last three weeks. Were they appropriate?*

→ *Discuss with your group how you might reduce the number of people attending each meeting and how to take care of people who are not invited.*

→ *Reduce the number of topics and increase the time for each by 30 percent.*

How we spend our days is, of course, how we spend our lives.

—ANNIE DILLARD, AMERICAN AUTHOR

5

Design Each Conversation

A meeting is, in essence, a series of conversations. And effective conversations are designed.

A leadership group in Brazil asked for guidance about conducting virtual meetings because they were rarely able to meet in the same location. After about sixty minutes of observation, I respectfully told them that virtual meetings would be difficult because they were not even close to being effective when they were in the same room. The number one problem, which is true of many meetings, was the lack of a clear and visible set of process steps for working through each of the topics on the agenda.

What are we trying to achieve in each topic?

Spending time designing each agenda item will make it easier to lead the discussion and allow people to contribute efficiently in a way that adds value.

For each conversation topic:

▶ **What are the desired outcomes?** Where do you want to be at the end of the discussion?

▶ **How much time is required?** Start by scheduling the amount of time the group will require if people stay on track and work effectively; you can always add five or ten minutes if necessary.

▶ **What input do you seek?** Being clear up front about what you want from the group will help keep the conversation focused.

▶ **What is the best process?** A clear path to follow allows the group to work through the discussion toward the desired result.

▶ **What preparation would be helpful?** Before the meeting, give participants the agenda and whatever information they need to be ready.

▶ **Who should lead the conversation?** Have someone who does not need to be heavily involved in the content but can focus on the process manage the conversation.

▶ **Do we need a visible process?** Groups larger than eight and groups meeting virtually benefit from visible process steps, such as a chart or handout.

Design the setup for each topic

The setup or introduction essentially lets people know where you are going and how you are going to get there. Some topics might require you to include more background in the setup, such as refreshing everyone on the timeline or how the budget process works.

Required setup elements for each topic:

▶ Why this topic is on the agenda

▶ Where you want to be at the end of the discussion

▶ What input you are seeking from participants

Optional elements for the setup:

▶ Information that will bring people up to speed

▶ Any concerns you (the leader) or participants might have coming in

▶ What permission you want to make it easier to lead the meeting

▶ The process steps to work through the topic

▶ Whether to track this conversation visually (charts/ whiteboard)

▶ How to capture and share this conversation (summary)

▶ The organizational leader's comments on the issue

Process steps map the path to follow

Following a specific set of steps makes it much easier to keep the conversation on track, and staying on track correlates with better outcomes and shorter meetings. Note that many topics do not need a formal process; instead, clear outcomes and an agreement to reach those outcomes in a specific amount of time will suffice. More complex agenda items will benefit from laying out a path to follow.

Six designs cover most topics

The following designs can be adapted to fit your topics. Follow them closely or allow them to inform your conversation without overly controlling it. Do what makes sense to you.

DESIGN ONE: STARTING A PROJECT

This is a time to go slow and get it right. Getting a project off the ground requires defining the overall project, including outcomes, timeline, milestones, and next steps.

1 **What have we committed to do?** Define the overall outcomes you have committed to achieve—the specific, measurable results that the project is designed to produce.

2 **What specifically are the outcomes?** Describe what success looks like—what you want to be true at the end of this project.

3 **What's the timeline?** From start to finish, set the important dates for accomplishing the steps that will help frame the project.

4 **What milestones make sense?** Determine the milestones that will give people a sense of progress and urgency from beginning to end.

5 **What will it take to produce this?** Determine what resources are required—everything that comes to mind—so they can be planned for early on.

6 **What relationships should we ensure are in place?** Define the relationships you will develop outside the project team with people who have something to contribute or a stake in the outcome.

7 **What actions will get us off to a great start? Who will do what by when?** Thinking of the next few weeks, define the set of actions that will give you a sense of momentum and get you off to a great start.

8 **When should we check in on progress?** Decide when and how often to check progress. Good project management includes follow-up and asking questions for clarification.

DESIGN TWO: CHECKING PROGRESS

Short updates can be done via email; this design is for a conversation to fully discuss where a project stands. Key projects deserve rigorous dialogue. You want the wisdom of the group to emerge, and that takes time.

1 **Where do we stand on this project?** Describe the current status of the project using key variables such as schedule, cost, resource allocation, quality, and so on.

2 **What questions do you have? What would you like to know?** Give everyone a chance to ask anything about the project or initiative.

3 **Is our progress where we intend it to be?** Assess project status in relation to intended goals and key targets, in particular where the project is behind schedule or facing difficulty.

4 **What concerns do we have, no matter how small?** Give people a chance to voice concerns or share problems that might otherwise remain hidden.

5 **What are the next steps? Who will do what by when?** Agree on a set of actions that will satisfy everyone in the group about what will be done next, including specific commitments from people and a timeline for completion.

6 **When does it make sense to schedule the next progress update?** Set a date to check on commitments and ensure continued progress.

7 **What are you taking away from this review? What should the project team feel good about?** Express value and appreciation.

DESIGN THREE: REQUESTING INPUT

One way to leverage the thinking of a group is to fully describe a problem or situation and then assign further work to a small group. When you need input from a larger group to describe or analyze a situation, these are the steps to work through:

1 **Here's the situation.** Describe the current situation or what has happened until now to bring everyone up-to-date.

2 **These are my thoughts and what I need from you.** Explain your viewpoint and define the input you need—ideas, questions, or concerns.

3 **What do you think?** Open the conversation to the group to get their input.

4 **What else?** Acknowledge what people say and keep asking for more until the group winds down.

5 **Anything else?** Check one last time for any other input. In particular, check with people who haven't spoken yet.

6 **Here's what I've heard.** Summarize what you heard and are taking away from the conversation.

7 **Here's what I suggest we do.** Explain what you plan to do with their input.

8 **Is everyone okay with what I'm planning to do?**
Check with the group to see if anyone has reservations about the next steps you propose.

DESIGN FOUR: RESPONDING TO A PROBLEM

When a problem has occurred and you need the wisdom of the group to help resolve it, these are the steps:

1 **What do we know?** Describe the situation thoroughly. Give an accurate picture of exactly what has happened, everything you know for sure.

2 **What questions need to be answered?** List the questions that need to be answered to fully understand the situation and gain new insight.

3 **What criteria should shape our response?** Determine a set of criteria to evaluate the options you will consider.

④ **What are our options?** Explore the options available for responding to the problem or identify people who may provide additional options.

⑤ **What else?** Open the conversation for additional thoughts.

⑥ **What are our next steps?** Decide what you will do next—actions to be taken, people who should be informed or consulted, and who will follow the progress of agreed-upon actions to ensure they get done.

DESIGN FIVE: MAKING A DECISION

When people speak about the need for transparency, one of the areas they are pointing at is decision-making. These are the steps for reaching a group decision:

① **This is the decision we face.** Clearly state the decision required so people know what they are determining in this conversation.

2 **Who has decision rights?** Discuss who has decision rights and the process to be used in making the decision.

3 **How should we decide? What are the objectives and criteria?** Outline the criteria for a successful outcome and how you will determine which option is best—what the decision must produce and what it will impact.

4 **What options do we have?** Define all the options available.

5 **What are the benefits and risks of each?** Outline the upsides and downsides associated with each option.

6 **What is our decision?** Make the decision.

7 **Is everyone okay with this decision? If not, what is in the way or missing?** Check for alignment, particularly identifying people who feel they cannot live with the decision, and continue until everyone is on board and will act accordingly after the meeting.

8 **How do we communicate this?** Identify people who would appreciate knowing what happened in this conversation and what you need to communicate.

9 **Who will do what by when?** Given the decision you made, define what you must do in the next two weeks—next steps, who will take these steps, and by what date.

DESIGN SIX: CREATING ALIGNMENT

This design may be the most useful of all the processes listed here. Management expert Peter Senge defines alignment as "what happens when people in a group actually start functioning as a whole." Alignment is correlated to engagement, which leads to inspired action. This is a process to master as a leader.

1 **Here's what I'd like to do and how I intend to implement it.** Describe your intended outcomes and the path you will use to produce those outcomes.

2 **What thoughts or questions do you have?** To find out what people are thinking, ask an open-ended question that allows them to express anything and everything.

3 **Is this clear? Does it make sense?** Ask whether they are clear about your intentions.

4 **Is it worth doing?** Ask if they see the value in this proposal.

5 **Is there anything in the way of your supporting this?** Ask people if they have concerns about the proposal.

6 **Is there anything missing that would help?** Once

you know what is in the way of their supporting the proposal, ask whether anything is missing that would make a difference to alignment if it were included.

⑦ If we address these items, will you align? Once you have the items identified in steps 5 and 6, ask the group whether, if you promise to address their concerns and requests, they are now able to align with the decision or plan.

TRY THIS

→ *For each meeting you prepare to lead, ask "How can I enhance it?"*

→ *Listen for the setup on every topic and assess whether it prepared the group to participate effectively.*

→ *Set aside fifteen minutes to prepare for each of your next five one-on-one meetings. See if you notice a qualitative difference in how they work.*

→ *Start on time and end early.*

Great meetings don't just happen—they're designed. Producing a great meeting is a lot like producing a great product. You don't just build it. You think about it, plan it, and design it.

—MICHAEL BEGEMAN, MANAGEMENT CONSULTANT, AS QUOTED IN *FAST COMPANY*

6

Lead Meetings Like a Pro

Everybody is talented,
original, and has something
important to say.

—BRENDA UELAND, AUTHOR AND JOURNALIST

A friend and client who is a senior manager in a Fortune 100 company received a promotion that jumped her over people with more experience and more knowledge in the function. Curious, she asked the CEO why she was chosen, and he replied, "Because you are the best person I've ever seen at managing the conversations in a meeting, and at this level, it's all about meetings."

The intent of this chapter is to make it possible for you to lead your meetings with the ease and grace of a professional facilitator, because leading meetings is a core competency for managers.

Whenever my friend led a meeting, she had three objectives in mind: accomplish the agenda, create a quality experience for everyone, and always be working on something that will improve how meetings are done in the future.

Objective One: Accomplish the agenda

Explain to your group how you intend to lead the meeting. Ask for the permission you need to manage the conversation, and suggest agreements for how the group will work together.

Permission changes everything

You know yourself and the group. What would make you more at ease and more effective in leading the meeting? Want to call on people? Get specific commitments? Then ask. This is an important part of setting up the meeting.

Remind the participants that they also have permission to ask questions at any time, to push back if they aren't clear, to ask for more time if necessary—in short, to ask for whatever they need to be effective in this meeting.

Lastly, ask for the help of the group on things you think are important, such as staying on track, getting more people into the conversation, or figuring out what to do next when the conversation bogs down. People will help if you ask, and it's nice to have them on your side.

Establish agreements

Agreements are guidelines you put in place to shape how you interact together. Having established agreements helps avoid common issues and provides permission to resolve issues when they do arise.

Here are four broad agreements for meetings:

1 Take care of yourself.

2 Ask questions at any time.

3 When people are talking, let's give each person our full attention.

4 If something doesn't work, let's talk about it.

These agreements are broad enough to cover almost anything, and they create an expectation that the meeting will be managed deliberately and thoughtfully. Adapt these agreements to match you and your group.

AN AGREEMENT ABOUT DISTRACTION

Too many of us sit in meetings with a roomful of people doing other work, having side conversations, or checking their devices. This trend toward constant access to technology needs to be stopped cold in its tracks. People think they can multitask effectively. They can't. It takes a bit of courage to push back, but meetings are too important. If you allow distractions in meetings, the entire purpose of the meeting is in jeopardy.

Here is how you might express this agreement in the setup for your meeting:

Within the agreement to take care of yourself, you certainly have my permission to leave the room at any time to check on your family or critical projects. I realize you may have calls you are waiting for or projects you are tracking. Please use your judgment.

That said, I would love your full attention when we are in the meeting, so please check your electronics at the door. I ask this for two reasons: because they are distracting to me and to others, and because your attention and listening matter to the quality of our work together. If you want to put your phone on vibrate, not a problem, unless it vibrates every five minutes. Exceptions are fine; patterns are troublesome. Also, if you want to take notes or use your tablet to refer to background information on our topics, please do so. I just ask that you resist the urge to check email or world news. Thank you.

Set up each conversation

Introduce each agenda topic in a way that brings people to the same starting place, including necessary background information, what you want to produce, what you want from people, and how the conversation will unfold to get you to the desired outcomes.

Often this last piece of setup—explaining the process steps to be followed—is missing, and a group will begin discussing a subject with no outline or plan for working through it. As a result, the conversation jumps all over the place, people begin making the same point over and over, and great points get lost.

Manage conversations so they stay on track

There are four primary reasons meetings go off track:

1 Lack of clarity about the process steps

2 People who speak too often or too long

3 Problem-solving and tangents that don't add value

4 Person leading doesn't make it a priority to manage the conversation in a deliberate way

Understand that, as leader, you can intervene if the conversation veers from the intended path, but you can also give participants permission to call attention to having strayed off topic:

▶ "I'd love to stay with this conversation, but I think we should get back to the agenda."

▶ "This sounds like an idea we should note and revisit at another time. Is that okay with everyone?"

Staying on track takes discipline, and few people make the effort to get it right. The process steps of the meeting design provide a clear track for the conversation to follow, and these might be included in the agenda, provided in a handout at the meeting, or written on a whiteboard to be a visible reminder of where you are in the conversation.

Closure wraps up the conversation

Closure is a final opportunity to make sure everyone is aligned and ready to proceed. There are five elements to effectively closing a conversation that bring a level of clarity about what happened in the meeting and what will happen next:

▶ **Check for completion:** *Is there anything else to be said or asked?* You don't want people leaving with something unexpressed.

▶ **Check for alignment:** *Is everyone okay with this?* If someone can't live with the decision, ask what is missing or in the way that, if addressed, would allow them to align with the group.

▶ **Confirm commitments:** *What happens next? Who will do what by when? How and when will we follow up?* Getting firm, clear commitments for action is the primary way to ensure progress.

▶ **Identify and express value:** *What are we taking away from this conversation?* Share what you gained from the meeting or how people affected your thinking on the topic and give others the opportunity to do so.

▶ **Express appreciation:** *Did anyone contribute to the conversation in a way that deserves to be highlighted?* Take a moment to thank those who went above and beyond to create an impact in the room.

If you stop reading this book right now and spend the next three weeks closing every conversation in a deliberate, thoughtful way, you will see immediate shifts in what gets done. This extends way beyond meetings. As a manager or supervisor, if you take time for this process step whenever someone meets with you one-on-one, the conversation and what happens as a result will improve dramatically.

Ensure progress between meetings

No matter how productive a meeting seems, if you do not complete the next steps generated during the meeting, not only will you not make progress, but it is discouraging to everyone. High-performing groups complete 85 percent of their action items between meetings. Most teams have a say-do ratio closer to 50 percent. Here are three ways to close the gap:

1 Emphasize making specific commitments with due dates.

2 Send out a meeting summary.

3 Ask someone to track and follow up on all actions.

The palest ink is better than the best memory.

—CHINESE PROVERB

DISTRIBUTE A MEETING SUMMARY

Ideally, meeting summaries keep your discussions, decisions, and actions alive and working after the meeting is over. Write and distribute the meeting summary within twenty-four hours, if not sooner. Share it with those who did not attend but who have a stake in the outcome.

Being able to represent what happened in a meeting to other interested people keeps them informed and aids progress. A single page will suffice for most meetings. The intent is not to re-create the discussion but to capture the key points and next steps for each topic to serve as a reminder for those in attendance and give those absent a sense of what happened and what should happen next.

FOLLOW UP ON COMMITMENTS

Good meetings and good intentions are not enough to ensure that the work produced during a meeting continues once it is over. Some managers are concerned that close follow-up might be interpreted as microman-aging. They don't want to be accused of not trusting people to perform. In reality, consistent follow-up is just good project leadership. Assign someone to check in at appropriate intervals to ensure the commitments will be kept as promised or reevaluated if something unexpected comes up.

Objective Two: Create a quality experience for everyone

High-performing teams do two things that most teams do not: create psychological safety for people to contribute, and insist on broad participation. Doing so creates an environment where people can feel they are unique, relevant, and included.

Getting broad participation is hard work. Even if you keep your group size below eight and you sched-ule more time for each topic, these common issues need to be overcome:

▶ A few people dominate the conversation.

▶ Most people walk into meetings feeling they don't have to speak.

▶ Meeting leaders have been told not to call on people directly.

Balancing participation levels doesn't mean everyone should speak the same amount. But it does involve both intervening when some people speak too often or too long and inviting people into the conversation who haven't yet contributed.

Letting people know at the beginning of the meeting that you would like broad participation will get you started. But eventually, you will need to call on people. It is worth the effort. People feel better about their contribution to the meeting and the team if they participate.

Include enough time on each topic to allow full

participation and slow down the conversation to include everyone. Call on people gently and strategically. Think each topic through ahead of time so you know whom you would like to invite into the discussion.

Make it safe to speak

People often leave meetings feeling as if they had something to contribute, yet they either didn't feel comfortable speaking up or, when they did, it seemed to have no impact. When you lead a meeting, you can ensure people leave feeling good about themselves and their participation. Making it safe begins with you. Work hard at being present. Be prepared so you can relax and enjoy your group. Then display empathy with attention and listening:

▶ Devote your attention to each person when they speak (set this as an expectation for the group).

▶ Let them finish without interruption.

▶ Check to see if they have anything else to say.

▶ Link their comments to the topic to show the value added to the conversation.

▶ Use their name and refer back to their comments later when it makes sense.

Invite people to speak

Most people have something to add…*if you invite them to speak*. Each person has a unique set of perspectives, experiences, and interests, but if they don't share them, you miss out on the value they could add. One way to change the pattern of not speaking is by inviting people into the conversation. The key word is *invite*. You're inviting them because you want to hear what they have to say.

Never put people on the spot. For example, if you notice they are multitasking, do not call on them to get their attention. **You always want people to feel good about being called upon to share their views.**

▶ "I want to hear from some people who haven't been in the conversation yet. Cindy, William, Chandra— you haven't been heard yet. I want to check in with you to see if you have any questions or comments. Then I'll come back to Damon and Inez, who have indicated they have something to add."

▶ "I want to be sure that anyone who hasn't spoken yet or who has additional comments can voice them."

You cannot count on people speaking up in a meeting. People are quiet for a variety of reasons— personal style, other people dominating a conversation, not wanting to make the meeting longer. Why doesn't matter. The point is, to have **truly effective** group conversations, you want to ensure that everyone who has something to say has the clear opportunity to be heard. The surest way to do that is to call on people directly. Calling on quiet people not only gets them into the conversation, it creates a sense of community and adds thinking that you would otherwise miss. To have something to say and not say it is a lonely place; call on people and give them a chance.

Leading a meeting intent on gaining broad participation and keeping it a safe place to speak will lead to engagement, inclusion, transparency, and alignment—things that everyone wants at work.

Objective Three: Get better as you go

Want to be remarkable? It takes patience, persistence, and practice!

In most areas of life—parenting, relationships, conversations, meetings—we aren't given time to practice. We are just expected to go out there and be good every day.

Still, getting better at something takes deliberate practice. And just as athletes often work on something during their games, you can do the same thing. Simply picking one idea or practice to focus on in each of your next ten meetings will do wonders. You will create an awareness for that idea immediately and, in two weeks, be able to apply it instinctively and naturally. Ten meetings or two weeks is a realistic time frame. That gives you six new tools in three months. You—and others—will notice the difference in your meetings.

That's the purpose of the Try This suggestions at the end of each chapter. Take these into your meetings and watch what happens. But don't limit yourself to these. Ask yourself or your group this question, and other ideas and practices will emerge: *What would you like to be true about meetings you lead or attend that is not true now?*

TRY THIS

→ *Tell the group what meeting skill you are working on.*

→ *Keep each conversation on track; ask the group to help you do so.*

→ *Notice who hasn't spoken and invite them to speak.*

To me, teamwork is a lot like being part of a family. It comes with obligations, entanglements, headaches, and quarrels. But the rewards are worth the cost... With a combination of practice and belief, the most ordinary team is capable of extraordinary things.

—PAT SUMMITT, BASKETBALL COACH

7

Participate to Have Impact

Personally, I've never found being on the sideline a successful place to be. The way that you influence these issues is to be in the arena.

—TIM COOK, APPLE CEO

I teach about twenty two-day workshops each year with about thirty-five people in each workshop. How often do you think that on the first day, someone walks up, introduces themselves, tells me they are looking forward to the class, and then asks if they can do something to help me get ready? Fewer than five—five out of seven hundred!

Most people walk into every meeting concerned only about themselves. *Where do I want to sit? Is there an outlet I can plug into?* If everyone walks in thinking only about themselves, your meetings will be ordinary at best.

Instead, walk into each meeting with a focus on being responsible for how it turns out, even if it's not your meeting. The mindset you have when you come into a meeting determines how you participate. Simply changing that mindset will do wonders.

If each of us decides that we have the ability to influence how meetings go, the path to remarkable meetings becomes easy. We all need to *choose ownership* for each meeting, even those we didn't organize. Any meeting we *attend* is one we need to *own*.

The choice is ours. We can either sit on the sidelines, wishing the meeting were over, or listen for what we might do to support the leader and other participants. In a busy world where we are all pressed for time, it only makes sense to participate in ways that produce the best outcomes for every meeting we attend.

Practice gracious listening

When a group pays attention to each person who speaks, safety, engagement, and alignment soar. Gracious listening has three components: being attentive, patient, and nonjudgmental.

Be attentive

Your focused attention is one of the critical variables in the success of any meeting, because **the level of listening and attention in the room adds to or detracts from the psychological safety participants feel**. If the group is attentive, it becomes easier for those speaking to be authentic and vulnerable—to say exactly what they think and feel.

Go into every meeting prepared to devote yourself to each person in the conversation. This level of attention will always add value to your meetings—in fact, to all your conversations. As you focus on listening in meetings, you will notice that most people end up speaking directly to you, making eye contact with you, because they naturally move their focus to the person paying attention to them. Being attentive means:

▶ **No multitasking.** Multitasking is a distraction both to the person doing it and to others. Speaking to a group that is not paying attention is hurtful. If you aren't paying attention, you send the message that you're not interested.

▶ **Leave technology at the door.** Keep only what you need for the meeting in front of you. The moment you look at your smartphone and read that text, you miss what is said. It also takes away from the experience of each team member who speaks.

Be patient

When you are listening, set aside your impulse to jump into the conversation. Wait for the other person to finish. Stop anticipating when you might get a chance to speak. Here's the hard part: don't step in when there's a pause. Wait and see if he or she has something more to add.

Be nonjudgmental

Being nonjudgmental is tough, because the human mind is wired to continually assess and make judgments. The mind is fast—very fast. Think about your ability to drive ten miles home and, when you get there, you

realize you don't remember making any of the turns along the way. On familiar roads, you assess and judge automatically, actually quite safely. But with people, that can get us into trouble.

There are ways to keep this judgmental mechanism at bay. Be curious. Remind yourself that the other person's views are as legitimate as yours. Give the person speaking the benefit of the doubt, and assume positive intent. When negative thoughts do occur, notice them and then set them aside and intentionally refocus on listening for clarity, understanding, and value. Watching your perspective here will pay dividends: if you choose to be gracious, you'll be gracious.

Speak in a prepared, focused way

Carefully prepare for every meeting. Be ready to speak. Your ideas, questions, and views are more unique than you think. In meetings, your speaking must be more focused than when hanging out with friends. Focused speaking reduces the time spent in meetings and ensures that people pay attention to what you have to say. It has four components: it is clear, concise, relevant, and respectful. And while we all want to speak well, remember that sincerity trumps polish. Trust yourself.

Be clear

Being clear starts with your intention to make your point and get out. Preparing your comments and questions for each agenda item before the meeting makes this easier. I know I'm asking for a lot here, but remember that meetings are leverage, and your participation can have a dramatic impact. Being remarkable takes attitude, preparation, and practice. This is one place to prepare.

Be concise

Get to the point quickly. Here are two tips:

► **Set up your speaking.** Saying "I have two points to make" not only tells people what is coming, it helps you organize your speaking.

► **Provide only enough explanation to achieve clarity.** Add extra detail or examples only if someone asks for them.

Don't wear out your welcome. No matter how brilliant you are, if you speak longer or more often than you should, people will lose respect for you.

Be relevant

Before you speak, ask yourself these questions:

► Will what I want to say add value and move the conversation ahead?

► Am I making a point or providing content that relates directly to the issue at hand?

▶ I disagree, but will it add value if I say so?

If the answer to any of these is no, then best not to speak.

Be respectful

Dialogue is made possible by people feeling safe. Respectful speaking lets people know there is room to see things differently. It is possible to be direct and candid without blaming or being confrontational or disrespectful. Just set up your comments and watch your tone of voice.

BUT WHAT IF I DO DISAGREE?

If you must disagree, do it in a way that shows respect. "I disagree!" is not a good entry statement for most people. Start by taking care of the other person. Make it clear that you understand the other point of view. Look for the value in his or her view and communicate it. Then you can express that you see it differently and ask for permission to explain.

▶ "Josh, I see the value in what you are proposing. If we go with your suggestion, do you have thoughts about how we get the faculty to be supportive?"

▶ "I see what you're saying, and I see it differently. May I tell you?"

Learn to hear and appreciate opposing views as a path to learning. While your first impulse might be to disagree, there are alternatives. You might ask the other person to continue speaking about the idea so you more fully understand it. You might simply withhold your contrasting view and see where the conversation goes. The trick is not to jump in automatically without consideration for where your disagreement might lead. As Dr. Wayne Dyer says, "When given the choice between being right and being kind, choose kind."

Participate in ways that add impact

There are seven ways to enhance the experience of the meeting for both the leader and other participants:

(1) **Support the person leading the meeting.** It makes a significant difference to anyone leading a meeting if people show support before it starts. Ask the leader how you can help before, during, or after the meeting.

(2) **Look out for other participants.** It's the responsibility of the person managing the conversation to make sure everyone has a good experience. But it's also a great way to contribute as a participant. Look for ways to improve other people's experience, such as noticing when they're interrupted and asking them to complete their thoughts.

(3) **Ask for what you need to participate fully.** You might not feel comfortable commenting on how the meeting is going, but you have the right to ask for whatever you need to be effective. If you need clarity, ask for it. If you need a chance to be heard, ask for it. Whatever you need, ask for it. Chances are someone else in the group will appreciate your asking.

4 **Be clear on outcomes and process.** Always check to see if you are clear about what outcomes are expected from the conversation and how you can contribute to getting there. This is a powerful way of adding value to the meeting. For example: *"Before we get into this topic, could you explain where you want to be at the end of the discussion?"* or *"Sarah, is there something specific you are looking for from us?"*

5 **Help keep the conversation on track.** When you notice that a conversation changes to something not directly related to the topic, you can call

attention to it with phrases such as: *"It seems that we've moved away from the topic. Do we want to stay with the current conversation or return to the original topic?"*

6 **Commit to specific actions.** Most people wait until they are asked to take on work. Be seen as someone who readily takes on work and then delivers. Make action statements, such as *"I am willing to complete that action by end-of-day Thursday."*

7 **Practice self-awareness.** Reflect on your speaking and how fully you listen and pay attention in meetings. Over time, the way you interact in meetings will improve. I often ask people to consider these questions:

i. *What do you do in meetings that probably doesn't work for others?*

ii. *What don't you do that might be helpful to others if you did?*

iii. What do people rely on you for?

iv. If you need feedback, who in your group would you ask?

TRY THIS

→ *Listen for what you appreciate or might learn about each person.*

→ *Listen for opportunities to improve the experience of others.*

→ *Notice when you have an idea or question, but don't say anything.*

Presence is more than just being there.

—MALCOLM S. FORBES, ENTREPRENEUR

8

Dealing with Ineffective Behavior in Meetings

Everything will be all right in the end. If it's not all right, it is not yet the end.

—SONNY, *THE BEST EXOTIC MARIGOLD HOTEL*

People are great…and sometimes difficult. Never is this truer than when you gather a group together for a meeting. Once you take on improving your meetings, you will be faced with behavior that doesn't work, and you'll need to decide what, if anything, you will do about it. The intent here is to review the underlying principles and ideas for dealing with ineffective behavior and provide enough examples so you can then map the ideas onto your own situation.

These are the most frequently expressed behavioral issues:

► People who continually interrupt

► People who speak more often than they should

► People who don't keep their commitments

Most people are aware of what they do that is difficult for others, and they prefer to be told. In fact, it's a gift when we do tell them, because awareness is the first step toward changing behavior. If you have your heart in the right place when you talk to someone, the conversation will work out. Set high standards for how to deal with people when they are being a bit difficult. Respond in a way that the other person will appreciate and that those watching will respect.

Choose an empowering perspective: Assume positive intent

Good people behave in difficult ways for lots of reasons. Why they do it is less important than the effect their behavior has on your meetings. But it is useful to remember that people do not plot out on their way to work how best to sabotage your meeting. So start by giving everyone the benefit of the doubt. Assume their intentions are good. We do this for ourselves, so let's extend the same courtesy to others.

Establish agreements up front

Agreements are designed to address patterns of behavior you can expect to run into when working with other people. If you review your working agreements at the beginning of each meeting, you will have less behavior to deal with and the safety to address it when it does happen.

Is the behavior a singular event or a pattern?

There are behaviors for which many organizations have adopted a "zero tolerance" approach—sexual harassment, for example, or illegal or unethical practices. Most meeting behaviors don't fall into this category. Occasional events, such as a cell phone ringing or someone having a side conversation, can be overlooked, but if these events become a pattern, then they are distracting and need to be addressed.

Three options for responding to behaviors that don't work

Within the context of meetings, you can use this model to help decide what, if anything, you will do. In dealing with behavior that doesn't work, you have three options for responding.

▶ **Option 1:** Let it go and make it work without taking it on. You simply wait for the behavior to stop, then restart as though it didn't happen.

▶ **Option 2:** Stop the behavior in the moment and ask for what you want. This allows you to take a stand for best conversational practices. The trick is to do this in a way that doesn't make someone wrong.

▶ **Option 3:** Speak with the person away from the group setting. After the meeting, let the individual know that the behavior was distracting, disempowering, and costly to you and the group. This is the most confronting of the three options, but it is the most likely option for producing a long-term change in the behavior.

Let's look at how each of these options might sound when dealing with typical complaints experienced in meetings.

People who continually interrupt

Interrupting is usually not an issue in small groups doing creative work. In larger groups, it can be seen as domination. The question is, does the interruption change the conversation, or does it shut down the contributions of the person speaking or of people who might have wanted to speak?

▶ **Option 1:** Let the person who interrupts finish his or her comments, then finish what you were saying or ask the person who was interrupted to finish. *"Sarah, I'm not sure you had a chance to finish your comments. Would you please make your points again?"*

▶ **Option 2:** Interrupt the interrupter; you can do this as the person leading the meeting or as a participant. *"Todd, I'd like to hold you back for a moment while Sarah finishes her thoughts."* Or *"Todd, I wasn't quite done. I'd like to finish, and then I'd love to hear your thoughts."*

▶ **Option 3:** After the meeting, thank them for participating, but correct the behavior. *"Todd, I appreciate your willingness to participate in the meetings. However, I don't think interrupting others is helpful. I want broad participation and a sense of safety in the group, and interrupting interferes with both of these. Would you please see if you can do it less often?"*

People who speak more often or longer than they should

Sometimes, people simply enter a conversation more often than is appropriate. It's as though the conversation is all about them and their views. It also doesn't work when people go on and on.

▶ **Option 1:** Listen and be attentive when anyone speaks. When it makes sense, start a discussion by calling on three people who tend not to join the conversation. This will change the pattern of the group.

▶ **Option 2:** Cut in and direct the conversation. *"Frank, if you don't mind, I'd like to hold you back for a bit while I get a couple of other people into the conversation."*

▶ **Option 3:** If the issue persists, take a firmer position and create an opportunity for the problem speaker to become solution focused. *"Frank, I would like the participation levels to be more balanced in our meetings. To achieve this, it would help if you waited on some topics until other people entered the conversation. Also, I would appreciate if you would help me out by noticing who might like to get into the conversation and invite them in."*

People who don't keep their commitments

We make progress when people agree to take action between meetings and then deliver. Being unreliable disappoints our colleagues and hurts our reputation.

▶ **Option 1:** This time, letting it go means not commenting on the lack of delivery. Simply ask the person for a new completion date. If this is a single event, this is the best option. We don't all keep our word at times. In fact, you might remind your whole team about the importance of doing what we say we will do.

▶ **Option 2:** If you feel there is a pattern developing in the team, then gently comment about each instance of non-delivery. *"Sonya, next time, will you promise to let me know if a deadline is in jeopardy so we can have a conversation?"*

▶ **Option 3:** If this becomes a trend and obstacle to team performance, set aside time to discuss it as a team. Acknowledge that everyone is busy and on multiple teams, and reaffirm the need to complete work as promised. Consider these questions:

→ *Does everyone feel they can say no or negotiate on action items?*

→ *Is it okay if we assign someone to follow up with everyone?*

→ *Is there something else we could do to make it easier to take on actions and complete them?*

The same conversation would work with an individual on the team. Take him or her for coffee and ask for input on how best to address the issue.

Listening to and addressing complaints

Perhaps the most common issue that all of us face—especially first-line supervisors—is dealing with complaints. The following process is simple and profound but rarely used because we haven't been trained in this way. We also have not been trained to listen and keep our advice and solutions to ourselves!

1. Let them know you are ready to listen. The process begins with someone who is upset or voicing a concern or complaint. Don't worry about how they express it. In fact, give up your right to be offended. If they are telling you, it's a gift!

2. Ask them to tell you about the issue, then listen until they have emptied out, said everything they can think of that's wrong. Just give them enough verbal and nonverbal feedback so they feel heard.

3 When they are finished, ask "What is your request? What would resolve this for you?" When someone comes to you with a complaint, it's important to understand that beneath every complaint is a request. Then go back and forth until you arrive at something you can do that will resolve the complaint in a way that also works for you.

Loyal, committed people complain. Learn to slow down, hear them out, and find out what they want. You'll earn their respect quickly.

Conducting difficult conversations is worth the effort

Some conversations are difficult because they don't work out well when we try to have them. Others seem so difficult or uncomfortable that we avoid having them. We think about having them, but we don't. But there are downstream costs to not voicing our concerns.

The first step is to sit down and think through the conversation and how you want it to go. Don't have the conversation unless you are committed to the person and are willing to stay with the conversation until it works out for the other person.

Think about how you'd like to be approached if someone has something to say that you're likely to take personally and get defensive about. Then approach the other person in the same way.

Here's how to proceed with a difficult conversation:

1 Ask for permission to talk to them about something.

2 Ask them to listen while you tell them what is bothering you.

3 Let them know what you are asking for going forward.

4 Ask them what they think about what you've said.

5 Thank them for being willing to discuss the situation.

You may never be comfortable having these conversations. With practice, you can become effective at them. That's what counts. One of my mentors consistently reminded managers: *"Everyone is a little bit scared and a whole lot proud. And if you remember this, you'll be better with people."*

I remain convinced that if we can talk, if we can

learn to trust ourselves, the other person, and the conversation, it will almost always turn out.

TRY THIS

→ *For two weeks, assume positive intent for every action or comment with which you disagree. See whether your response changes.*

→ *Don't complain without sharing what would resolve the issue for you.*

→ *After having a difficult conversation or listening to a complaint, reflect on what you said and how you said it, taking note of your insights.*

→ *Notice when blame is present in a conversation. Think about how that might have been avoided. Apologize if appropriate to do so.*

If you have some respect for people as they are, you can be more effective in helping them to become better than they are.

—JOHN W. GARDNER, AMERICAN AUTHOR AND EDUCATOR

Conclusion

Effective meetings are within reach. Leaders can dramatically shift how meetings are run at your company, which will improve both project execution and employee engagement. Individuals can improve their influence and impact by sharpening their process skills.

I hope by reading this book you've learned that rather than dreading your meetings, you can simply get better at leading them. Here are six reasons why doing so is a worthwhile investment of your time:

1 **You'll set yourself apart.** The ability to manage

conversations so that they are productive, inclusive, and focused on getting work done is an organizational skill that transcends expertise. Being really good at a core discipline (say marketing, business development, or social media) is important, but being an expert only gets you so far. If you can add the ability to facilitate conversations to your repertoire of skills, you'll add more value to your organization.

2 **You'll gain stature.** Your colleagues will respect your ability to make their time in meetings productive, even more so if you can manage the conversational processes with very little attention on you or your views. You are not doing this to get noticed, but it never hurts to be known for having a critical skill set.

3 **You'll create productive relationships.** The entire process of determining what should be on the agenda and interacting with colleagues about the best way to have a successful meeting gives you insight into what matters to people. Relationships are built on a series of conversations where people can express themselves fully and be heard. If you can do this, you'll build a network that you can depend on outside the meeting as well.

4 **You'll enhance your powers of observation and learn to stay out of the conversation.** Managing a meeting requires careful attention to the dynamics in a room—for example, whether someone needs to be brought into the conversation or an action item needs to be assigned or the discussion has gone off track. Facilitating a meeting also requires learning to withhold your own ideas and questions and focus on the input and thoughts of others. Many of us need practice at interrupting less, listening more deeply, and resisting the urge to focus a conversation on our own views or

experiences. These are important leadership skills in and out of meetings.

5 **You'll become valuable beyond your own group.** If you become known in the organization as someone who can manage conversations effectively, you'll likely be asked to help with other meetings. You may not be interested in becoming a professional facilitator, but even leading one or two meetings a month for other parts of the organization will build your network and knowledge of other functions.

6 **You'll contribute to your boss's success and respect.** Offering to design and lead the next meeting for your manager is a gift in several ways. Many managers simply don't have the time to determine what needs to be on the agenda and how best to get the broad participation required for alignment. With you facilitating the discussion, the boss can be completely attentive without the distraction of keeping the conversation on track. And being able to focus intently allows the manager to pick up on the nuances people express, verbally and nonverbally, and to listen for the organizational perspective or any background the group needs.

Beyond improving your own skills and advancing your career, getting better at running meetings will be dropping a pebble in the pond of ineffective meetings—it will ripple outward. When you begin to deliver meetings that people look forward to and benefit from, others will realize your organization is not doomed to have wasteful, ineffective meetings and may be inspired to follow your example.

Get started

Whether you are the manager who calls meetings, a project leader who runs team meetings, or someone who attends meetings as a participant, the action items throughout this book will help make your conversations—and therefore your meetings—more effective.

There is no need to implement every idea all at once. Meetings are plentiful. Deliberately choose where to put your attention in upcoming meetings. Find one idea that resonates with your own experience and work on it for two weeks or the next ten meetings. Once you have that idea working for you, find another. Just take it meeting by meeting, idea by idea.

The first thing to do is to *start* and then watch your meetings become extraordinary.

How to start

Here's my list of ideas to begin working with:

▶ Notice who is not yet in the conversation and invite them to speak.

► Keep the conversation on track; ask the group to help you do so.

► Make sure each commitment has a completion date.

► Start on time and end early.

► Let people know what meeting practice you are working to improve.

**Try not. Do. Or do not.
There is no try.**

—**YODA,** *THE EMPIRE STRIKES BACK*

Acknowledgments

There are three people without whom this book would not have happened. Gwil Evans was the first client who embraced the idea of designing meetings not only for outcomes, but also to change the experience of meetings for the participants. Cheryl McLean is a jack-of-all-trades editor who saw the possibility of a book that would be both useful and readable. Lastly, Cindy, my wife, has been helping me refine the ideas and my training programs for a very long time. We have debriefed more days of training and meetings than we can remember.

From an idea point of view, I owe a great deal to

Tim Gallwey, Michael Nichols, Dale Carnegie, Malcolm Gladwell, Geoff Colvin, and countless other authors and teachers who contributed to my thinking on individual and group effectiveness.

I'm indebted to the clients who asked questions and put these ideas into practice where they could be tested and refined.

My thanks go also to Amy Gallo at *Harvard Business Review*, whose incisive editing helped me strengthen my message about meetings since the original book was published.

About the Author

PHOTO © CINDY OFFICER

PAUL AXTELL provides consulting and personal effectiveness training to a wide variety of clients, from Fortune 100 companies and universities to nonprofit organizations and government agencies. With an engineering degree from South Dakota School of Mines and an MBA from Washington University in St. Louis, Paul's early career was spent in manufacturing, engineering, and management.

For the last twenty years, Paul's focus has been devoted to designing and leading programs that enhance individual and group performance, whether for line workers and admin staff at a manufacturing plant or regional managers and CEOs in global corporations. He has gathered decades of insights into a succinct collection of fifteen strategies in a small but powerful booklet, *Being Remarkable*. It is the centerpiece of the Being Remarkable series, a training program complete with a facilitation guide for trainers as well as a personal workbook for individuals or small groups to work through independently. The series also includes access to Paul's video introductions to the journey toward being remarkable as well as to each strategy.

His book *Meetings Matter: 8 Powerful Strategies for Remarkable Conversations* offers a deeper dive into improving meeting competence. It won numerous awards, including the Nonfiction, Benjamin Franklin, Eric Hoffer, and Nautilus Book Awards, and is the foundation of this text.

A new edition was published recently of his book *10 Powerful Things to Say to Your Kids: Creating the Relationship You Want with the Most Important People in Your Life*, which applies the concepts behind his work to the special relationships between parents and children of all ages. It was named Best Parenting Book of 2012 and has since been translated into Korean, Vietnamese, Chinese, Arabic, French, and Spanish.

Paul lives with his wife, Cindy, in Minneapolis and Phoenix.

NEW! Only from Simple Truths®

IGNITE READS
spark impact in just one hour

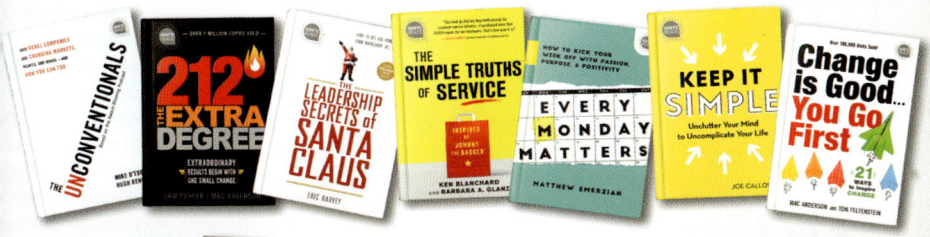

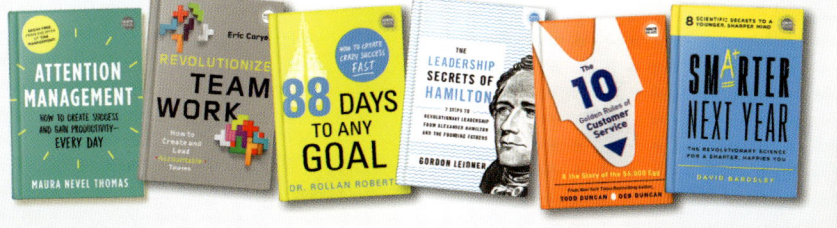

IGNITE READS IS A NEW SERIES OF 1-HOUR READS WRITTEN BY WORLD-RENOWNED EXPERTS!

These captivating books will help you become the best version of yourself, allowing for new opportunities in your personal and professional life. Accelerate your career and expand your knowledge with these powerful books written on today's hottest ideas.

TRENDING BUSINESS AND PERSONAL GROWTH TOPICS

 Read in an hour or less

 Leading experts and authors

 Bold design and captivating content

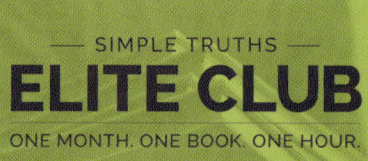